Fragments in a Glass Bowl

Fragments
in a Glass Bowl

Don McLagan

For Jady
With appreciation
— Don McLagan

MMXIX

Library of Congress Control Number: 2019913805

ISBN: 978-1-692-82333-7

Edited by Jennifer Leonard
Printing by Tisbury Printer
Book Design by Janet Holladay

Cover & author photographs by Edwina Rissland

Don McLagan
donmclagan@gmail.com

For Barbara
Marnie and Christopher

She felt... how life, from being made up of little separate incidents which one lived one by one, became curled and whole like a wave which bore one up with it and threw one down with it, there, with a dash on the beach.

—Virginia Woolf, *To the Lighthouse*

Contents

I

II

III

IV

I

Sunday School Bible

Awarded to ten-year olds so they can learn
who begat... who begat... who begat whom,
that *a virgin will conceive,* that *Jesus wept.*
Our teacher is the ferocious
Mr. McBride whose avalanche eyebrows
furrow and shudder. His lips pinch
as he describes fires of damnation
that will melt our skin and bubble
our bodies if a drop of alcohol
passes our lips.

Amid underwear, socks and LP records
the Book trails along to college
where it languishes. I read Nietzsche
and Kierkegaard. Old McBride dies.
Join a fraternity, tap one keg, then
another. The musty Bible follows.
We marry, move, move again,
have kids, retire. Now it sits gray
and unopened on the credenza.

Our son works on Step 2, explores
his higher power. Wants to share
spirituality with his son who is ten.
Wants to buy a Bible. Dusting mine,
I find a surprising number of markers.
I'll give him this one.

Tiger

When it's dark
and I have to put my feet
on the bare floor, I know
huge claws lurk,
yellow eyes see.

The sheet makes
a flimsy shield
from the tiger who lives
under my bed. He crept in
just after mom moved me
downstairs — to my big-boy
room. Out of my sister's room,
away from all three of them,
even the bathroom — all
upstairs now.

Thin protection, but if,
if I cover my whole head
except for a small breathing hole,
he won't see, won't find me —
the tiger waiting for my bare feet
on his bare floor.

How the Toilet Seat Got Its Crack

His mom's speech
is well-rehearsed: *When you feel it,*
hurry! To the bathroom. Lower
your pants, pull down your trainers.
Quickly. And she always finishes,
Don't forget to lift the seat!
because she hates the surprise
of a wet skirt and bottom.

I imagine all this
is a lot to remember — quickly,
for a young boy, when he's in a hurry.
And the specter he sees — that seat
poised above eye-level, threatening
like a Kohler guillotine. Him
with his delicate member stretched,
thin-necked, over the threshold. *Please,*
don't let it drop!

And I can imagine
the thrill of victory — of feeling it.
The sprint to the bathroom. The successful
lowering of pants and trainers. Seat up.
The stretch over the porcelain goal line.
And no chop of the guillotine. Exuberance

like the scoring football player
he watches with his dad on Sundays.
So now it's time for his celebration,
his own version of the touchdown
slam! Except, there is no football,
just that raised toilet seat.

Echo Rock

Swishing grass doesn't grow
on the granite mound, it's bare
as Popi's bald spot. That's the rock
where my week-end sister and I
toss our hollers down the field,
tilt our heads and know for certain
our hellos will return.

When we run to that rocky spot,
dewy grass tickles our knees
and Nana calls, *Girls, watch out for ticks!*
Tic, toc, they're just bugs! Anyway
the dogs race ahead clearing our way
with their furry legs. She and I always
get to the rock together.

Popi says our voices hit the trees
and bounce back. We watch each other
to shout at the same time, super loud.
Do the trees jiggle, their leaves tingle,
do we make dents in the bark?
They come back together, our voices.

On Sunday night, my sister
goes back to her other Mom.
She doesn't like to leave.
Sometimes she cries out,
but there is no echo.

New Pants

*Those pants are frayed
at the cuffs,* Mom says, *Threadbare
in the seat.* Dad says nothing.
He often says nothing. I watch her
give him a few bills from the kitty
in the kitchen drawer. *Go to Grant's.
Get yourself new slacks.*

Outside, I catch pop-ups
off the garage roof, my cracked mitt
trails dried leather chips
with each catch of the ball.

Then he returns. But the bag
reads Nassiff Sporting Goods,
not W. T. Grant. *On sale,*
dad says, taking out, handing me
a new Wilson "Ball Hawk" glove
which gives a big league *thwock*
when he throws me the ball.

There are rules

she says when there are six of us
and she closes the bedroom door.

Boy, girl, boy, girl. Sit cross-legged.
On the wood floor. The girls
seem to know. *So you can't choose*
where the milk bottle stops.

She has buckteeth and plays the flute.
I play the clarinet. We're in the band.

The closet is the place. Awfully
dark. *Leave the door*
open a crack. Of course
I have kissed before!

In the closet. Together.
Touch just her lips. Her lips
like on the flute. Are seconds
allowed? Her lips are soft.

On the way out, I wipe the bottle
with my shirt. Return it
to the milk box on the porch.

For My Roommate, I Say to the Pharmacist

Of course, he says. The man in the white coat
has heard all the variations, and he dispenses
safe sex without judgment. However, he does have
questions — single, 3-pack or dozen-box? Tipped
or regular? Lubricated or plain? His queries
keep me at the window like a schoolboy
at confession. I just want Trojans and to be gone.

Baritone voice, guitar, All-Prep swimmer,
my roommate has reason and opportunity
for protection, but he's shy about the store.
My girlfriend is Catholic, but I want
to prove myself, at least by buying.

The interrogation is over. No one I know
comes into the store. When I return,
my roommate is out — swimming, playing
his guitar, singing to the tall blonde girl? I know
he's not at the library. So I leave the box of eleven
tipped and lubricated condoms in plain sight
on the center of his desk. He won't miss
the twelfth which fits snugly in my wallet.

Galoshes

When I asked for combats, Mom
bought galoshes. The tough guys
wore combat boots. Military '43s
with brass double-buckles
to belt in pant legs — jumpsuits
for paratroopers, jeans
for snowballers. *Galoshes*

she said, *are better.* Slip on
over school shoes, real rubber
for waterproofing, adjustable fasteners
for snow pants. *Dickies,*
the snowballers taunted. *Dic-
kie,* they called me too. Sixty

years beyond, I lace the metal
hooks and grommets of my Sorels —
confident the tough leather uppers
and Aero-Trac outsoles
will never be called Dickies.

Mirror

Losing its silver backing,
the old glass mixes opaque
and reflection, the way brown spots
appear on clear skin.

      I study Dad, watch him watch
      himself shave. He lathers my face
      with his badger brush and warm soap.
      Gives me his bladeless razor so I
      can be old enough to shave.

      Mom checks her hair. Pauses
      while fluffing the curl,
      That's not gray is it?

As long as Mom and Dad were old,
I was not.

Conversation with Ducks

Paired for life doesn't mean
suicide in Lane 5, I warn.
The mallards squat comfortably
in Steamship Authority waiting lot
where vehicles and impatient
drivers queue for the ferry.

Our car is in Lane 6. I watch
a red GMC swerve out of 5 into 4
to hurry around the ducks, and onto
the ferry. An SUV follows, kids
pointing. And quickly, others.

My wife and I will be married
for fifty years. Our anniversary
is next month. If we die together
our ashes will be combined. Neither
of us wants to be second.

The ducks cock their heads,
look at me, eye-to-eye. We seem
to agree. *Not here, not today*.
They waddle into Lane 6,
and settle with us in standby.

Getting a New Puppy in Old Age

You and I will wash each other's ears
though I will swab while you
clean with your tongue. We can be
two ends of the same short line,
but must learn not to tangle. Neither
of us will tell Mom
about the last piece of cake.

Yes, you win the cold nose
contest, and we know each
other's smell. But we have agreed,
nosey is not a good thing
in polite society. Right?

At night, your place is the kennel
behind the couch in the kitchen.
But in the evening, after supper
and our walk in the field, it's okay
to climb on the couch for a snuggle.
And if it should happen
that I become alone and sad,
you can sleep in my bed.

Annual Physical

Bend over, the doctor says, *drop*
your shorts. I'm stuck replaying
the work up —
>   the nurse notes   *you've*
>   *lost two inches in height*
>   she tests both ears
>   with the otoacoustic emitter
>   I frown and ask   she checks
>   *yes* the emitter is working
>   she retries   still I hear
>   nothing —

Now!
The doctor wants my attention.
Lean on the exam table. I do.
He puts on prophylactic
gloves. Lubricates
his index finger. Swipes
like a hurried barkeep
stirring a martini. *No*
prostate, he observes.
No. There is no olive
and no gin.

Round Birthdays

A decade holds all the nights
and days of a teenager. For an infant,
a decade is enough time to learn
all the fingers on both hands — Yes,
there are ten. Round birthdays
do not end in slanty numerals,
but only when the pen finishes
a complete circle.

Bearing the freight of our lives,
decades rumble on. The date
of *old age* rises like a helium balloon
tied to a child's wrist. Round birthdays
become crossings, signals to distant
friends and those in daily touch: Take note!
There's a person here. She has lived,
and does live. Here. With us.

Woman in a Straw Hat

She sits by herself, at the left end
of the bench. The seat faces the bay

where sunshine pairs water and sky
in blue calm. She doesn't look there

but down towards her hands, folded
in her lap. White hair is gathered

into a tidy bun below her straw hat. Its brim
rounds up like a worn smile. She wears

a blue-and-white plaid shirt that is too big
and is collared for a man's neck.

Tide and clouds drift, unbidden, without
hurry. Sun warms the tender place

at the back of her neck where the hair
is lifted. On the bench, her body

leans to the right, as if toward a shoulder.

II

Son Like an Avalanche

At first, a few flakes stick
on the weathered ridge.
Sun melts, night freezes.
Crystal bonds grow, fasten
crag and outcrop. More snow,
wind packs, a cornice builds.
Cliff and ice fuse — hard,
fragile.

With a crack like the start
of a long race, crystal
bonds break. Unbound,
ice and pieces of rock careen
and catapult, leap and tumble
energized and separate.
On the ridge, the crag remains
fissured and bare.

Phone Call

Like the tolling bell
of an old clock that aches up
to that pointy hour again,
the phone rings. *Dad, I need*
help. I need to go to rehab.
Today. It's the same call
as twelve years ago. Yes.
I'll pay.

There's nothing more for me to do.
His friend will take him. His wife
will deal with the six kids. The old clock
ticks long minutes, but the day is bright
with fall leaves, so I walk.

While the dog dances, sadness
weighs like a soaked cloak.
I am grateful for the simple task
of collecting the dog's shit
in a disposable plastic bag.

Reciting *Ulysses* at 3 am

Frayed ends dangle
      and twist. Will he find work?
            Stumble again? No thread

of daylight to weave the warp of worry.
      If I get up, the floor will be cold,
            the bed light thin. Must sleep.

Must be ready. Drowse tangles
      like kelp around an overturned sailor.
            The poem memorized for calming —

start again, at the top. *It little profits*
      that an idle king…I mete and dole…
            They are not subjects. They are

my grandchildren and I am no king. Frayed
      ends. *This is my son,*
            mine own Telemachus.

Mine own son. In the dream,
      the path is iced, boots slip —
            there is no grip coming down.

Can't Park There

Outside of Al's Wine & Spirits
is a restricted parking space.
My son can't park there —
he doesn't warrant a blue card
dangling from the mirror
or a special license plate.
Doesn't matter. My son
shouldn't park anywhere
near Al's.

There is no white cane
for what he has. *Drunk. Addict.*
User. Freak. The words stain
like a bad tattoo. *A disability*
is what someone has, not what
someone is. I swish that phrase
around my tongue like mouthwash.

Cocktail Party

The twins got into Harvard.
Well, do you know that Facebook
is recruiting our daughter? Mayor —
my boy is running for mayor!

He didn't go to college. Our son
doesn't have a job. No one
is recruiting or voting for him.
His mom and I are groceries
and rent for his family.

What he is, our son, is alive,
and 90-days sober. He's moved
away, to a farm in Alabama
to repair his family
and himself. But that's not
what we will talk about
at the cocktail party.

Tossed Coin

When he gathers his life, I hurry
difficult nights into the past. Again,
I dream of possibilities. See my son.
See him smile. And I lock
worry in the box of *before*.

Addiction, the stubborn bully,
waits its moment. One day
at a time is a slow, exposed path.
Acceptance is a difficult balance,
a tossed coin landing on its edge.
Today is a good day.

III

Gilbert

Temperature is 62,
the grizzled face with gravel voice
announces. Monument to the new day,
Gilbert has proclaimed weather and sports
from his seat on Boston Common for thirty-nine
years. 6 am joggers, dog walkers and early-bird
professionals stride past. A few regulars share
a little something for me, the Beacon Hill Town Crier,
for his assuring presence, for the comfort
of knowing that over the hours of their sleep,
nothing happened so important as to interrupt
the earth's roll toward the sun.

Across Charles Street amid the well-tended
tulips of the Public Garden, George Washington
prepares to gallop down Commonwealth Avenue.
Bronze statues honor him and six other white men.
The 6am-ers pass these monuments as well.
But the icons are silent while the raspy
voice of the black man on the Common
continues. *Bruins win. Four-to-two.*
Rain at 3 o'clock. Bring your umbrella.

Eduardo Writes His Poem

Words are noise in my ears,
an explosion of sticks
on the board. The visitor
with a book reads, then writes
on the white board — white board
for white kids. Taylor, always
first, has his hand up. Book-man
glances at me, calls on Taylor.

Book-man says something ... *write*
... *"Conflict"... five minutes.*
I know about five-minutes-es —
I study them on the clock.
After twelve of them, the class
is over. Miss James

who always sits behind me
writes *Con - flict*
on the top line of my pad.
She whispers, *What does "Conflict"*
make you think of?

Most of the kids are writing
with yellow pencils. I like the smell

of my yellow pencil when I grind it
in the sharpener. Miss James
reminds me, *Eduardo,*
can you write something?

Taylor has a plastic green pencil.
It's always sharp. He just twists it.
The clock hand gets near the twelve.
She urges again, *Conflict* ...
It sounds like mom shouting.
I write on the second line

Me.

Nose-to-Nose

Her lip curls, his back is up.
Frozen. Faceoff. Concentration
mirrored. Dog and skunk
locked on each other. Locked
in place. A whisker-twitch
from explosion.

In traffic one car drifts, clips
another's mirror. They stop. Words.
One jumps the other's hood,
bangs windshield, grips wipers
as the other drives off. Bang/
bang. Fast/slow. Bang/bang. Fast/
slow.

In the yard, dog and skunk
quiver, appraise, eyes
still locked. Then each
steps back. The dog comes
when she's called. The skunk
carries on rooting for grubs.
Three miles down the road
both men are arrested.

It Shouldn't Rain on Memorial Day

Wet flags drip and don't flutter.
Long socks squish in Scout shoes.
Soldiers from old wars are cold.
Trumpets burble as they play
the Sousa marches.

Moms keep kids dry, at home
watching Nickelodeon, where no vets
march. No one offers poppies, collects
donations with a slot-top can.

The kids don't ask
why does he limp and will there be another
war? *Oh — and where is Afghanistan?*
Will Dad need to carry a gun?
Will I?

Tilt-a-Whirl

Three dollars, three minutes,
the barker tempts. Tilt-a-Whirl
spins us against its cylinder wall.
Girls scream, guys try to muscle
their arms, no one can move legs.
It tilts — stomach floats to throat.

The solstice is so much easier.
Spinning a thousand miles an hour
is like standing still. Nothing
at our back to keep us upright
except atmosphere.

Vacation comes for school kids,
sun warms the sand and our bare feet,
strawberries pop red among low green leaves,
blueberries plump for picking, and the fair
comes to the vacant lot.

Do you feel the shift -
the tilt going the other way?
The warm days shorten now.
Take the ride of your life,
the barker calls, *Hurry.*
Hurry.

Waiting for the Hurricane

Across the harbor, the light
built for night and storm
is not yet lit. Fishermen
cast into the smokegray —
but the fish are gone
       to deeper water.

Tremble is in the hydrangea
and in the lace
of the honey locust. Breeze
tucks the water,
       pleats it ashore.

Toward the buoy,
the last moored boat
tugs and pitches
       in the gust.

The chairs are stowed
except this one. The dog rests
at my feet, but her eyes slit
open and her nose
       is into the wind.

September

Wind from the north clears
the laze of summer. Seaweed
collects on the lee shore
and squishes cold under bare feet.
Across the sound, Victorian hotels
emerge as small, white vacancies.

Oh, there's still prance
in the dog's step, peaches
plump and drizzle, and corn
carries sweetness from the farm.

But the porch door is closed,
the morning swim replaced
by a fire at night, and once again
yellow busses scoop kids from the curb.

Free Speech

*Political spending is a form of protected
speech under the First Amendment.*
— Citizens United vs. Federal Election
Commission, January 21, 2010

Who can hear a heart beat
while electronic funds thrum?
When change jangles in private
pockets? As air whooshes
from dark money vaults?

What is the sticker price
of a Senator? The cost
to elect a Rep? How much for a decal
on the Presidential limousine?

Do voices just rustle
like spent leaves in winter?
Scuttle like a sand crab? Keen
like a dog's low plaint
during thunder?

What did we sell
when the Court
gaveled the bench
like the auctioneer's mallet
at Sotheby's?

November 9, 2016

The flutter and shade of summer
is gathered and piled. All season,
leaves of oak, walnut, and maple
stirred in the wind. Disconnected

and brittle, they lie in a raked mound
of ocher and umber. Wind of early
winter provokes their spent shapes
and casts them, like angry ballots,

against my window. Sitting
inside with the morning news
on my lap, I see all of this
and none of it.

DELUXE INFLATABLE
ARM BANDS

Two chambers, more safe,
calls the crone peddling pink floaties,
Insurance, each arm, two chambers.

Four times Aya's mom seals her lips
around the stiff plastic valves. Tight,
so that no puff escapes
the thin plastic cavities. Drawing
again and again on that deep
motherplace where lungs,
heart, and uterus lie so close.
What a desperate legacy,
she thinks as she lifts
Aya aboard the King
of the Shore's leaky raft.
What a meager dowry —
just the breath of my body
in four plastic bags.

Whiteville

In my high school class
were 623 white kids and
one black girl. Her picture
is in the yearbook.

My college class had two black kids.
They didn't join our fraternity.

About Trayvon,
Obama said, "If I had a son…"
My son was arrested, released.
The judge was white, like my son.

There are no
black families
in our neighborhood. None
in my writing group. One
black woman works
in our tech company.

What does she feel like?

I don't know what it is to be black.
I don't even know what it is to be white.

Scraps

Crow-pecked words settle
in the litter ignored
by scavenging badgers.
Caulking guns rust
among broken hyphens.
Empty bags rustle
past discarded titles.
Spoils of dinner molder
on crumpled edits. An old man
with spectacles and a stubby
pencil pokes the refuse
looking for metaphors.

IV

Wasque

This is a place of pixel elements —
grains of sand, sea spray, salted wind —
the material of an impermanent beach.
Today sea and sky are the color
of shadows. A southwest gale rakes
the sea into spume and punches it ashore.
The island stretches twenty miles east
to this spot and shoreline blunts
the running waves. But here
the beach takes a sharp angle,
and the sea rips.

Rips the sand which sloughs
and sluices. Rips itself, churning
bait into broth for bluefish and bass.
The flung pellets sting fishermen,
level departing footprints, and leave
only the swirl of elements.

Reason for ER Visit:

On my 6 am walk with the dog,
we come across a seal pup shrouded
in a net on the beach. Was it curiosity,
an accident, some morsel of food
lodged in the green cords? Whatever,
I'm prepared with Swiss Army knife
and Boy Scout sense of duty.

Here's what we're going to do, I explain
looking into the seal's liquid eyes
and reach to cut him loose. He looks
at the blade approaching his neck
and bites. Thumb, fingers, knife –
all in his mouth, like some unfortunate
mullet. Spits them out. My hand
is punctured and bleeding. He
is still trapped. We're committed.

Approach again, this time from behind.
No more explanation. Stand on
the still-in-place net to hold him down.
At the back of his neck, I slip the knife
under one strand. Cut. Then another,
safely now.

The lines free, he waddles off. No
Thanks, I'll pay it forward, or even
Good-bye. Just back to the sea
and then gone.

Close Hauled

She sweeps past to the lee.
Over my gaff rig, her great main
sculpts like a bird in space. Sixty
years ago Olin Stephens designed
Columbia to defend the America's Cup.
She swept the Brits in four straight.
She is here. Now.

A hundred years ago, Nathaniel
Herreshoff designed the boat I race
so boys could learn to sail in the bluster
of Buzzards Bay. But, in this moment
between the red nun and the lighthouse,
Columbia and my small boat
share the channel. The same water
buoys both of us. The same wind
fills our sails. And in this brief passage,
we are both close hauled
and on the same tack.

In the Video

the dog quivers, leaps
into the ball's arc, into the pool.
A hard tail swoosh and she heads
to the steps. Surely the black lips
around the yellow ball smile.

Click the control panel, reverse
the tracker to the moment of launch —
forelegs stretch, rear legs extend,
ears lift, eyes lock on the splash
of her target. That's it! — that leap
of untethered joy. Freeze it.
Save this digital pulse.
It can restart the heart.

Lighthouse at Cape Poge

Isolated at the elbow of the thin-armed
cape, the tower was lifted by helicopter
and set again away from the surf. Visitors
climb the steep stairs, then a steeper ladder
to the lens, and wonder how a single bulb
no bigger than an eye can warn
all the way to the mainland.

On the bluff, a rough-cropped path
leads through red cedar and poison ivy
to the edge. Below lies the old foundation,
lowered intact by pall-bearing sand.
There is no sound but the whir
of mosquitos. Beyond
the sea waits curled and whole.

Nor'easter

East grips the wind
like an unruly child.
Writhing north,
the wind rankles
and foams the sea.
Towards the south,
it drizzles and droops.
East does not loosen
her hold. Sullen clouds
and cheerless rain
persist like melancholy.
Even the bright sand
of the beach is sodden.

Trail to the Beach

Conch shells dangle in branches,
like a carillon of unclappered bells.
Was it a family on a warm day
that built this improbable belfry?
So many limbs. So many shells.

At the edge of Cape Poge Bay,
where the trail becomes beach,
shells and stones are vulnerable
to storm wind and high tide.

Our son and his wife built their six kids
into a family. In a court on the mainland
at the end of next week, our son
and his wife will divorce.

I gather six flat stones,
pack sand by the trail sign,
and build a wobbly steeple,
a piece of green sea glass
buried underneath.

Reading Her Email on My Laptop

How to respond when she says, *Popi,*
I have nowhere else to turn. She persists,
It's 1700 miles to see my mom who's got
cancer. The tires aren't safe. The kids
need glasses. My cards are maxed.
               And I love her kids,
        my step-grandchildren.

What do I say when I've have already
financed her divorce from our son? Given her
another big check last month? When I know
she will need more next month?
               And the market is up,
        my stocks are doing well.

Across the table, my wife says, *No!*
Her asking is awkward. It demeans
our relationship, and my wife is right
about awkward and demeaning.
               So what
        do I type

when she writes, *I'm trying like hell,*
but I need help.

Chores

She looks over her shoulder
into our kitchen from her nest
in the ivy. We fuss over who
cooks, does dishes, takes out
the trash. At first the bird
skittered. Now she settles
for the long, two week sit
until her azure eggs crack
and become beaks hungry
for bugs and grubs.

Or maybe it's a *he*.
The guidebook says robins
share the sitting and foraging.
It's a guidebook for humans.
The birds already know.

Peppermint Ice Cream

There's no more peppermint
at the Candy Bazaar. Oh there's
chocolate, vanilla, even snickerdoodle.
But peppermint is out of stock,
off the list, gone from the display
where cool pink and red chips
brought drool to hot tongues.

Fourth of July cones
have all been licked, fuchsia drips
bleached from T-shirts, and the last
errant scoop slurped
from the sidewalk by the dog.

Yes, peach
had a brief season,
but it was too — well,
adult. And pumpkin,
even with sprinkles,
lacks fire power.

Only peppermint
recalls the blaze of summer,
electricity in the first frozen
bite, expeditions after supper
on vacation with mom and dad.

And now, there is no
peppermint ice cream
at the Candy Bazaar.

Do you like this with the gold pants?

She's going to a reunion
with her partners. Their firm
became famous. She —
the girl with freckles
and red hair, an MBA
and a motorcycle. The one
who shared high school
and all her college dates
with me. I say, *I really like, um*

your black pants
with that jacket.
She nods, changes,
shows off the outfit
now with black pants.
When I nod, she smiles
and says, *Now that's*
why I have a husband.

Fragments

In the pre-dawn, a shard
glimmers in the fleck
and mottle of sea wash.
The piece has no curve, no
raised letters. But stone-worn
and matte-edged, it has its own
form. I'll bring it home

              and place it
where I've arranged your mug,
packet of French Roast, spoon
and one Splenda. When you
come to breakfast, still fuzzy
with sleep, you'll say, *Ooh,*
you found sea glass for me!
and add it to the kaleidoscope
of given and received fragments
in the clear glass bowl.

The Hermit Crab Has
No Zillow Listing

The crab endures no septic
inspection, no fire alarm tests.
He suffers no closing with agents,
lawyers, and deeds. His is
a most simple transaction.

He has no frenzy in the attic,
no decisions about grandma's
bureau, the chewed teddy bear,
photos in the kitchen drawer.
He makes no promises
to stay in touch. Just scoots

to the next shell. Leaves
in a dumpster no LP records,
rusted pliers, deflated pink swan,
Monopoly set missing its thimble
and flat iron. He has no wife
to say we have lived our whole life.
Together. Here.

Leaving

Mist soft as gray silk
settles and clings
to the field's round
and rise like a lover's blouse.
Through tall grass puffed
with seed, the path worn
by so many jaunts coaxes one more
circuit. The dog bounds with the bliss
of just-finished breakfast,
our walk, and the possibility
I will throw the ball. She
doesn't think about moving
away, and the last time
clinging like soft gray silk.

New Driver's License

In my wallet, the driver's license
says I am now a Florida resident.
A hologram ensures it's official.
The license says I can drive
any non-commercial vehicle
under 26,000 pounds past Disney
on the I-4. From Amelia Island
to St Augustine on A1A.
All the way down the Keys
on Route 1. The photo
shows me smiling:

      was I thinking
about the nor'easter we missed
on the Vineyard? Or Fenway pitchers
blowing on October-cold fingers?
Yes. We are
here, and we will
go barefoot on the beach in February.
Though each morning, I look
for messages from Boston
in my email, and wait
for the *Times* in the driveway.

Downwind

And in the sailfull moment
when the stern lifts
and tiller is still,

when the rise of wind and wave
are stalemate
with gravity,

in that breath-
caught, heart-
paused moment,

before plunging
down
the slippery breast,

a breath of shy
happiness whispers,
I am here. I never left.

Acknowledgements

Each poem in this book has been improved in workshops with the Bookstore1 Poets, Concord Poetry Center, or the Martha's Vineyard Poets Collective, and by audiences who have listened with open ears and hearts. Jennifer Leonard deserves particular recognition for her careful and creative editing.

Grateful acknowledgement is made to the *Vineyard Gazette* where the poems "September" and "Tilt-A-Whirl" first appeared.

Proceeds from the sale of

Fragments in a Glass Bowl

are donated to

MARTHA'S VINEYARD MUSEUM

Home to whaling captains and poets, Martha's Vineyard is an island of rich history, remarkable places and diverse people. The Martha's Vineyard Museum inspires all people to discover, explore and strengthen their connections to this Island and its diverse heritage. Of particular importance to this book and its author is the Museum's *Rose Styron Garden of Poetry and Human Rights.*

For more information about the Museum, call 508-627-4441, link to www.mvmuseum.org, or visit in person at

Martha's Vineyard Museum
151 Lagoon Pond Road
Vineyard Haven, MA
02568

Made in the USA
Lexington, KY
07 November 2019